contents

M000011759

For pattern inquiries, please visit: www.go-crafty.com

sun kissed

Yarn ④

Bernat®*Sheep(ish) Stripes*™ by Vickie Howell 2.4oz/70g skeins, each approx 137yds/123m (acrylic/wool)
• 1 skein in #03006 Citrus(ish)

Hook

• Size I/9 (5.5mm) crochet hook
  OR SIZE NEEDED TO OBTAIN GAUGE

Additional

• Yarn needle

MEASUREMENTS

12 x 24"/30.5 x 61cm

GAUGE

14 sts x 8 rnds = 4"/10cm over FPdc, BPdc Rib St.
TAKE TIME TO CHECK YOUR GAUGE.

STITCH GLOSSARY

FPdc (front post double crochet) Yo, insert hook from the front around the back of the post of the st in the row below to the front and pull up a loop (3 loops on hook), yo and pull through 2 loops, yo and pull through 2 rem loops.

BPdc (back post double crochet) Yo, insert hook from the back around the front of the post of the st in the row below to the back and pull up a loop (3 loops on hook), yo and pull through 2 loops, yo and pull through 2 rem loops.

TC (twin cluster) [Yo, insert hook in next sc, yo, pull loop through, yo, pull through first 2 loops on hook] 3 times in next sc, yo, pull through all 7 loops on hook.

COWL

Ch 72. Join round with sl st in first ch.

Bottom Band

Rnd 1 Ch 3 (counts as dc), dc in next ch and every ch around. Join rnd with a sl st in top of beg-ch.

Rnds 2 and 3 Ch 3 (counts as FPdc), BPdc in next dc, *FPhdc in next dc, BPdc in next dc; rep from * around. Join rnd with a sl st in top of beg-ch.

Body

Rnd 4 Ch 1, sc in next dc and each dc to end. Turn.

Rnd 5 Ch 4, sk 1st sc, * TC over next 3 sts, ch 2; rep from *, ending with TC over last 3 sts, ch 1. Join rnd with a sl st in top of beg-ch.

Rnd 6 Ch 1, sc in ch-1 sp, *sc in top of TC, 2 sc in 2-ch sp; rep from * around. Join rnd with a sl st in top of beg-ch.

Rep rnds 5 and 6 until piece measures 8½"/21.5cm.

Top Band

Rep rnds 2 and 3, then dc in each st around. End off. ■

ribson girl

Yarn (4)

Bernat® *Sheep(ish) Stripes*™ by Vickie Howell 2.4oz/70g skeins, each approx 137yds/123m (acrylic/wool)
• 5 skeins in #03001 Punk(ish)

Hook

• Size H/8 (5mm) crochet hook
  OR SIZE NEEDED TO OBTAIN GAUGE

Additional

• Yarn needle

MEASUREMENTS

14 x 32"/35.5 x 81cm

GAUGE

9 sts x 8 rows = 4"/10cm over FPdc, BPdc Rib St.
TAKE TIME TO CHECK YOUR GAUGE

STITCH GLOSSARY

FPdc (front post double crochet) Yo, insert hook from the front around the back of the post of the st in the row below and pull up a loop (3 loops on hook), yo and pull through 2 loops, yo and pull through 2 rem loops.

BPdc (back post double crochet) Yo, insert hook from the back around the front of the post of the st in the row below and pull up a loop (3 loops on hook), yo and pull through 2 loops, yo and pull through 2 rem loops.

COWL

Ch 121. Join rnd with a sl st in first ch.

Rnd 1 Ch 3 (does not count as dc throughout), dc in next st and each st around. Join rnd with a sl st in top of beg ch-3.

Rnd 2 Ch 3, *FPdc in next 2 sts, BPdc in next 2 sts; rep from * around. Join rnd with a sl st in top of beg ch-3.

Rep rnd 2 for FPdc, BPdc Rib St until piece measures 14"/35.5cm.

End off.

marmalade

Yarn (4)

Bernat® *Sheep(ish)*™ by Vickie Howell
3oz/85g skeins, each approx 167yds/153m
(acrylic/wool)
• 2 skeins in #00013 Pumpkin(ish) (A)
• 1 skein in #00014 Coral(ish) (B)

Hook

• Size K/10½ (6.5 mm) crochet hook
  OR SIZE NEEDED TO OBTAIN GAUGE

Additional

• Yarn needle

MEASUREMENTS

10 x 30"/25.5 x 76cm

GAUGE

8 sts x 9 rows = 4"/10cm over FPhdc/BPhdc
seed stitch and double strand of yarn.
TAKE TIME TO CHECK YOUR GAUGE.

NOTE

Cowl is worked with 2 strands of yarn held
together throughout.

STITCH GLOSSARY

FPhdc (front post half double crochet) Yo,
insert hook from the front around the back
of the post of the st in the row below to the
front and pull up a loop (3 loops on hook),
yo and pull through all 3 loops.

BPhdc (back post half double crochet) Yo,
insert hook from the back around the front
of the post of the st in the row below to the
back and pull up a loop (3 loops on hook),
yo and pull through all 3 loops.

COWL

With double strand of A, ch 60. Join rnd
with sl st in first ch.

Rnd 1 Ch 2 (counts as hdc), hdc in each
ch around—60 hdc. Join rnd with sl st in
top of ch-2.

Rnd 2 Ch 2 (counts as FPhdc), BPhdc,
*FPhdc, BPhdc; rep from * around. Join rnd
with a sl st in top of ch-2.

Rnd 3 Ch 2 (counts as BPhdc), FPhdc,
*BPhdc, FPhdc; rep from * around. Join rnd
with a sl st in top of ch-2.

Rep rnds 2 and 3 until piece measures
3"/7.5cm from beg.

Cut A, join one strand each of A and B held
tog (A/B).

Rep rnds 2 and 3 until piece measures
7"/18cm from beg.

Cut A/B, join double strand of B.

Rep rnds 2 and 3 until piece measures
10"/25.5cm from beg.

End off. ■

cable gal

Yarn (4)

Bernat® *Sheep(ish)*™ by Vickie Howell 3oz/85g skeins, each approx 167yds/153m (acrylic/wool)
• 2 skeins in Turquoise(ish) #00017

Hook

• Size I/9 (5.5mm) crochet hook
  OR SIZE NEEDED TO OBTAIN GAUGE

Additional

• Yarn needle

MEASUREMENTS

Cicumference 60"/152.5cm
Width 5½"/12.5cm

GAUGE

18 sts x 7 rows = 4"/10cm over pattern stitch.
TAKE TIME TO CHECK YOUR GAUGE.

NOTES

Can be worn long as an eternity scarf, or doubled as a cowl.

STITCH GLOSSARY

BPdc (back post double crochet) Yo, insert hook from the back around the front of the post of the st in the row below and pull up a loop (3 loops on hook), yo and pull through 2 loops, yo and pull through 2 rem loops.

FPtr (front post triple crochet) [Yo] twice, insert hook from the front around the back around the post of the st in the row below, pull up a loop (4 loops on hook), [yo and pull through 2 loops on hook] twice, yo and pull through rem 2 loops.

COWL

Body

Ch 23.
Row 1 Dc in 4th ch from hook and in each ch to end. Turn—20 dc.
Row 2 Ch 3 (counts as dc), dc in next 6 dc, sk 3 dc, FPtr in next 3 dc, FPtr in 3-sk dc, dc in last 7 sts. Turn.
Row 3 Ch 2 (counts as hdc), hdc in next 6 dc, BPdc in next 6 sts, hdc in last 7 sts. Turn.
Row 4 Ch 3 (counts as dc), dc in next 6 dc, sk 3dc, FPtr in next 3 dc, FPtr in 3 sk dc, dc in last 7 sts. Turn.
Row 5 Rep Row 3.
Rep rows 2–5 for pat st until piece measures approx 60"/152cm from beg.
End off.

FINISHING

Fold piece in half length-wise and seam ends to make a circle.

Edging

Join yarn at top edge seam.
Rnd 1 Ch 2, hdc evenly around entire top edge. Join with a sl st at top of beg ch-2. End off.
Rep for bottom edge. ■

grandana

Yarn (4)
Bernat® *Sheep(ish) Stripes*™ by Vickie Howell 2.4oz/70g skeins, each approx 137yds/123m (acrylic/wool)
• 2 skeins in #03003 Night(ish) (A)
Bernat® *Sheep(ish)*™ by Vickie Howell 3oz/85g skeins, each approx 167yds/153m (acrylic/wool)
• 1 skein in #00014 Coral(ish) (B)

Hook
• Size I/9 (5.5mm) crochet hook
  OR SIZE NEEDED TO OBTAIN GAUGE

Additional
• Yarn needle

MEASUREMENTS

Circumference at upper edge 21"/53.5cm

Upper edge to point 18½"/77cm

GAUGE

16 sts x 5 rows = 4"/10cm worked over dc.
TAKE TIME TO CHECK YOUR GAUGE.

COWL

With A, ch 4.

Row 1 2 dc in 4th ch from hook. Turn—1 dc cluster.

Row 2 Ch 3 (counts as dc), 2 dc in same st as ch, ch 1, sk 1 dc, 3 dc in top of beg-ch. Turn—2 dc clusters.

Row 3 Ch 3 (counts as dc), 2 dc in same st, ch 1, 3 dc in next ch-sp, ch 1, sk 2 dc, 3 dc in last dc (top of beg-ch here and throughout). Turn—3 dc clusters.

Row 4 Ch 3, 2 dc in same st as ch, ch 1, *3 ch in next ch-sp, ch 2; rep from *, end 3 dc in top of last dc. Turn— 4 dc clusters.

Cont in this manner, inc 1 dc cluster every row, 21 times more—25 dc clusters.

Cut A, join B.

Next row Ch 2, hdc in next 2 dc, *2 hdc in next ch-sp, hdc in next 3 dc; rep from * to end. DO NOT TURN.

Create Closure

Ch 6. Join rnd with sc into top of beg-ch. *Ch 6, sk 2 on opposite side, sc in next st; rep from * 2 times more, ch 6, sk 1 on opposite side, sc in next st.
End off.

FINISHING
Fringe

(make 25)

Cut 4 strands of yarn 38"/96.5cm long. Holding strands together, fold in half. Insert hook through beg ch of one row at side edge of cowl. Lay folded point of strands over the hook. Pull the yarn through cowl edge from back to front, just enough to create a loop. Set aside crochet hook and use your hands to fold loop over edge of cowl and pull ends of yarn through loop. Pull until taught.

Attach 25 fringe evenly to cowl edges, placing one in every other row. ■

rainbow night

Yarn 4

Bernat® *Sheep(ish)*™ by Vickie Howell
3oz/85g skeins, each approx 167yds/153m
(acrylic/wool)
• 1 skein each in #00001 Black(ish)
(A), #00015 Red(ish) (B), #00014
Coral(ish) (C), #00012 Yellow(ish) (D),
#00020 Chartreuse(ish) (E), #00017
Turquoise(ish) (F)

Hook

• Size H/8 (5mm) crochet hook
  OR SIZE NEEDED TO OBTAIN GAUGE

Additional

• Yarn needle

MEASUREMENTS

9½ x 27"/30.5 x 68.5cm

GAUGE

13 sts x 7 rows = 4"/10cm over pat stitch.
TAKE TIME TO CHECK YOUR GAUGE.

COWL
Body

With B, ch 90.
Row 1 Hdc in 3rd ch from hook, and in
each ch to end. Turn—88 hdcs.
Row 2 Ch 2 (does not count as hdc), hdc in
same st as ch and in every hdc across. Turn.
Cut B, join A.
Row 3 Sl st in turning ch, sl st in next st,
ch 4 (counts as tr), tr in next 2 sts, tr in
first sl st (creates cross stitch), *sk next
hdc, tr in next 3 sts, tr in sk st; rep from *
to end.

Row 4 Rep row 3.
Cut A, join C.
Rows 5 and 6 Rep row 2.
Cut C, join A.
Rows 7 and 8 Rep row 3.
Cut A, join D.
Rows 9 and 10 Rep row 2.
Cut D, join A.
Rows 11 and 12 Rep row 3.
Cut A, join E.
Rows 13 and 14 Rep row 2.
Cut E, join A.
Rows 15 and 16 Rep row 3.
Cut A, join F.
Rows 17 and 18 Rep row 2.
End off.

FINISHING

Seam side edges to create cowl. ■

netfix

Yarn

Bernat® *Sheep(ish)*™ by Vickie Howell
3oz/85g skeins, each approx 167yds/153m
(acrylic/wool)
- 1 skein in #00003 Grey(ish) (A)
- 1 skein in #00020 Chartreuse(ish) (B)

Hook
- Size I/9 (5.5mm) crochet hook
  OR SIZE NEEDED TO OBTAIN GAUGE

Additional
- Yarn needle

MEASUREMENTS
8 x 30"/20.5 x 76cm

GAUGE
4 ch-5 sps x 8 rows = 4"/10cm over mesh pat.
TAKE TIME TO CHECK YOUR GAUGE.

COWL
With B, ch 40.
Row 1 Sc in 8th ch from hook (1 ch-5 sp
and 1 sc made), * ch 5, sk 3, sc in next ch;
rep from * to end. Turn.
Row 2 *Ch 5, sc in ch-5 sp; rep from * to
end. Turn.
Rep row 2 for mesh pat until piece mea-
sures 9"/23cm from beg.
Cut B, join A.
Cont in mesh pat until piece measures
30"/76cm or desired length from beg.
End off.

FINISHING
Match short ends, then flip one end over to
create mobius; sew tog. ■

navy daisy

Yarn

Bernat® *Sheep(ish)*™ by Vickie Howell
3oz/85g skeins, each approx 167yds/153m
(acrylic/wool)

- 1 skein in #00022 Navy(ish) (A)
- 2 skeins in #00004 White(ish) (B)
- 1 skein in #00012 Yellow(ish) (C)

Hook

- Size H/8 (5 mm) crochet hook
  OR SIZE NEEDED TO OBTAIN GAUGE

Additional

- Yarn needle
- 4 Buttons
- Sewing needle and thread

MEASUREMENTS

10 x 33"/25.5 x 84cm

GAUGE

1 Daisy Square = 4"/10cm.
TAKE TIME TO CHECK YOUR GAUGE.

COWL

Daisy Square

(make 12)
With C, ch 4. Join rnd with a sl st in first ch.
Rnd 1 Ch 1 (counts as sc), 7 sc in center
ring—8 sc. Join rnd with sl st to top of
beg-ch.
Cut C, join B with sl st in any sc.
Rnd 2 Ch 3 (counts as dc), 4 dc in same st
as ch 3, remove loop from hook, insert hook
from front to back in top of ch 3, put loop
back on hook, yo, pull through both loops
(petal made), ch 3, *5 dc in next sc, remove
loop from hook, insert hook from front to
back in top of ch 3, put loop back on hook,
yo, pull through both loops, ch 3; rep from *
6 times more. Join rnd with a sl st in top of
beg ch-3—8 petals.
Cut B, join A.
Rnd 3 Sl st to first ch-3 sp, ch 3, 2 dc, *
(2 tr, ch 2, 2 tr) in next ch-3 sp (corner
made), 3 dc in next ch-sp; rep fr * 2 times
more, * (2 tr, ch 2, 2 tr) in next ch-sp.
Join rnd with a sl st in top of beg ch-3.
Rnd 4 Ch 2 (counts as hdc), hdc in same
st as ch and in next 3 sts, (2 hdc, ch 2, 2
hdc) in ch-2 sp, *hdc in next 6 sts, (2 hdc,
ch 2, 2 hdc) in ch-2 sp; rep from * 2 times
more, hdc in last st. Join rnd with a sl st in
top of beg ch-2. End off.

FINISHING

Join squares in 2 rows of 6 squares each
as foll:
Join A at corner of one square. Ch 3, sc in
corner of 2nd square, * ch 3, sk 1 hdc on
1st square, sc in next hdc, ch 3, sk 1 hdc on
2nd square, sc in next hdc; rep from * until
all squares are attached both vertically and
horizontally.

Edging

Join B to corner with sl st to work edging
along one short side as foll: Ch 2, *hdc in
each hdc, 2 hdc in ch-2 sp, (hdc, ch 2, hdc)
in ch-3 sp, 2 hdc in ch-2 sp; rep from * to
next corner, 3 hdc in corner ch-2 sp.
Cont in this manner around until all 4 edges
have been worked. Join rnd with sl st to top
of beg ch.
Next rnd Ch 2, hdc in next st *(hdc, ch 6,
sl st) in next st to form button loop, hdc in
next 6 hdc; rep from * twice more, (hdc, ch
6, sl st) in next st to form last button loop,
cont around, working 1 dc in each hdc, and
2 hdc in each ch-2 sp.

Picot Edge

Turn to work picot edge along one long side
of cowl as foll: Ch 4, * sl st in 3rd ch from
hook, sc in next st, ch 3; rep from * to last
st along top edge, sc. End off.
Join B with sl st to corner of opposite long
side and rep picot edge.
Sew on buttons to correspond with loops. ■

summering

Yarn (3)
Bernat® *Cotton-ish™* by
Vickie Howell 2.4oz/70g skeins, each
approx 282yds/258m (cotton/acrylic)
• 1 skein in #85700 Jade Jersey

Hook
• Size G/6 (4mm) crochet hook
  OR SIZE NEEDED TO OBTAIN GAUGE

Additional
• Yarn needle

◼◼◼▭

MEASUREMENTS
8 x 24"/ 12.5 x 61cm (excluding tassels)

GAUGE
16 sts x 18 rows = 4"/10cm worked over sc.
TAKE TIME TO CHECK YOUR GAUGE.

STITCH GLOSSARY
hdc-cl (half double crochet cluster)
[Yo, insert hook in st and pull up a loop]
4 times, yo and pull through all loops on
hooks, ch 1 to close.

COWL
With A, ch 132. Join rnd with a sl st in
first ch.
Rnd 1 Ch 1, sc in next ch and every ch
around—95 sc. Join with sl st in beg ch.
Rnd 2 Ch 1, sc in first sc, * ch 3, sk 2 sc, 4
hdc-cl in next sc, ch 3, sk 2 sc, sc in next sc;
rep from * around, end last rep ch-4.
Join rnd with a sl st in beg ch.
Rnd 3 Ch 1, sc first sc, *ch 3, sc in 4 hdc-
cl, ch 3, sc in next sc; rep from * around,
end last rep ch 3. Join rnd with a sl st in
beg ch.
Rnd 4 Ch 6 (counts as dc, ch 3), sk first
sc, sc in next sc, *ch 3, 4 hdc-cl in next sc,
ch 3, sc in next sc; rep from *, end ch 3, dc
in last sc. Join rnd with a sl st in 3rd ch of
beg-ch.
Rnd 5 Ch 1, sc in 1st sc, *ch 3, sc in next
sc, ch 3, sc in next 4 hdc-cl; rep from *
around to last sc, ch 3, sc in last sc, ch 3, sc.
Join rnd with a sl st in beg ch.
Rnd 6 Ch 1, sc in 1st sc, *ch 3, 4 hdc-cl
in next sc, ch 3, sc in next sc; rep from *
around. Join with a sl st in beg ch.
Rep rnds 3–6 six times more.
Next rnd Ch 1, sc in same st as ch and in
every st around. Join rnd with a sl st in beg
ch. End off.

FINISHING
Fringe
(make 7)
Cut 3 strands of yarn, 18"/45.5cm long.
Holding strands tog, fold in half. Insert
hook through RS and out through WS of
"seam" created by first st of each rnd; lay
yarn at folded point over the hook. Pull
the yarn through, from back to front, just
enough to create a loop. Set aside crochet hook and use your hands to fold loop
over edge of project and pull ends of yarn
through loop. Pull until taught.
Attach 7 fringe evenly along "seam." ◼

boho cowl

Yarn (4)

Bernat® *Sheep(ish) Stripes*™ by Vickie Howell 2.4oz/70g skeins, each approx 137yds/123m (acrylic/wool)
• 2 skeins in #03002 Earth(ish)

Hook

• Size H/8 (5mm) crochet hook
  OR SIZE NEEDED TO OBTAIN GAUGE

Additional

• Yarn needle

MEASUREMENTS

Circumference 26"/66cm
Length 13"/33cm

GAUGE

13 tr x 3 rows = 4"/10cm.
TAKE TIME TO CHECK YOUR GAUGE.

STITCH GLOSSARY

FPdc (front post double crochet) Yo, insert hook from the front around the back of the post of the st in the row below and pull up a loop (3 loops on hook), yo and pull through 2 loops, yo and pull through 2 rem loops.

BPdc (back post double crochet) Yo, insert hook from the back around the front of the post of the st in the row below and pull up a loop (3 loops on hook), yo and pull through 2 loops, yo and pull through 2 rem loops.

COWL

Bottom Rib Band

Ch 100. Join rnd with a sl st in first ch.
Rnd 1 Ch 3 (counts as dc), dc in next ch and every ch around. Join rnd with sl st to top of beg-ch—100 dc.
Rnds 2–5 Ch 3 (counts as FPdc), BPdc in next st, *FPdc, BPdc; rep from * to end. Join rnd with sl st to beg-ch.

Body

Rnd 6 Ch 4 (counts as tr), 9 tr, ch 10, sk 10, [10 tr, ch 10, sk 10] 4 times. Join rnd with sl st to top of beg-ch.
Rnd 7 Ch 4 (counts as tr), tr, [ch 2, sk 2, 2 tr] twice, ch 10, sk ch-10 sp, *2 tr, [ch 2, sk 2, 2 tr] twice, ch 10, sk ch-10 sp; rep from * 3 times more. Join rnd with sl st in top of beg-ch.
Rnd 8 Ch 4 (counts as tr), tr in next 3 sts, ch 2, sk 2, tr in next 4 sts, ch 10, sk ch-10 sp, *4 tr, ch 2, sk 2, 4 tr, ch 10, sk ch-10 sp; rep from * to end. Join rnd with sl st in top of beg-ch.

Rnd 9 Ch 4 (counts as tr), tr, [ch 2, sk 2, 2 tr] twice, ch 4, dc around ch-10 sp from THREE rows below, ch 5, *2 tr, ch 2, sk 2, 2 tr, ch 2, sk 2, 2 tr, ch 4, dc around ch-10 sp from THREE rows below, ch 5; rep from * to end. Join rnd with sl st in top of beg-ch.
Rnd 10 Rep rnd 6.
Rep rnds 6–10 once more.

Top Rib Band

Rep rnds 2–5 once, rep rnd 1 once.
End off. ■

my notes